LIFE IN A POND

By Adam Hibbert

Gareth Stevens

Please visit our Web site www.garethstevens.com. For a free color catalog of all our high-quality books, call toll free 1-800-542-2595 or fax 1-877-542-2596.

Library of Congress Cataloging-in-Publication Data
Hibbert, Adam, 1968-
    Life in a pond / Adam Hibbert.
       p. cm. -- (Nature in focus)
    Includes index.
    ISBN 978-1-4339-3411-7 (library binding) -- ISBN 978-1-4339-3412-4 (pbk.)
    ISBN 978-1-4339-3413-1 (6-pack)
    1. Ponds--Juvenile literature. 2. Pond ecology--Juvenile literature. I. Title.
QH98.H53 2010
578.763'6--dc22   2009038718

Published in 2010 by
Gareth Stevens Publishing
111 East 14th Street, Suite 349
New York, NY 10003

© 2010 The Brown Reference Group Ltd.

For Gareth Stevens Publishing:
Art Direction: Haley Harasymiw
Editorial Direction: Kerri O'Donnell

For The Brown Reference Group Ltd:
Editorial Director: Lindsey Lowe
Managing Editor: Tim Harris
Editor: Jolyon Goddard
Children's Publisher: Anne O'Daly
Design Manager: David Poole
Designer: Lorna Phillips
Picture Manager: Sophie Mortimer
Picture Researcher: Clare Newman
Production Director: Alastair Gourlay

Picture Credits:
Front Cover: Shutterstock: (main image); Mircea Bezerghaeanu (background);
BRG: Tim Harris: 21; FLPA: Ron Boardman, Life Science: 10; Hans Dieter Branl: 7bl; B. Borrell Casals: 9t: Foto Natura Stock: 14, 17, 20; ImageBroker: 16; Derek Middleton: 18; Mark Moffet/Minden Pictures: 11; Alwyn J Roberts: 22; Michael Rose: 12; istockphoto: .13, 19, 30; John Pitcher: 29; Jupiter Images: Stockxpert: 15t; Shutterstock: 31; Bruce Amos: 24; Stephen Bonk: 26; Seve Byland: 23; Steve Estvanik: 5; Cindy Haggerty: 9; Jubal Harshaw: 8; Kavram: 4; Sergey Mikhaylov: 7br: B. Neeser: 25b; Orionmystery@flickr: 15b; Lori Skelton: 28; Robert Venn: 6b; Shannon Workman: 3
All Artworks Brown Reference Group

Manufactured in the United States of America
1 2 3 4 5 6 7 8 9 12 11 10

CPSIA compliance information: Batch #BRW0102GS: For further information contact Gareth Stevens, New York, New York at 1-800-542-2595.

Contents

Ponds Around the World

There are freshwater ponds all over the world. Many creatures live their whole lives in one pond; others just visit in search of food or water. Ponds are small self-contained worlds. All the types of life in ponds rely on one another for food, oxygen, and shelter. In this book, you will visit a North American pond and see what lives there.

Most ponds form where rainwater has filled natural dips in the land.

In tropical rain forests, water lilies grow leaves up to 6 feet (1.8 m) across and have flowers more than 1 foot (30 cm) across.

The leaves on these water lilies are about the size of dinner plates.

Pond Life

cattails

mink

duckweed

dragonfly

stickleback

newt

Canadian pondweed

Ponds are more sensitive to change than lakes. They are shallow and small, so water temperatures can swing up or down by 20°F (11°C) in one day.

Pond life has to be able to survive if the pond should dry to a soggy patch of mud in the heat of summer. It must also cope when a layer of ice seals the pond off from the air in winter.

Ponds also need a good mix of minerals and oxygen in the water. If the pond water were absolutely pure and clean, nothing would be able to survive in there.

PLANTS AND ALGAE

Plants and **algae** provide pond animals with oxygen and food. Trees at the edge shelter the pond from sunshine.

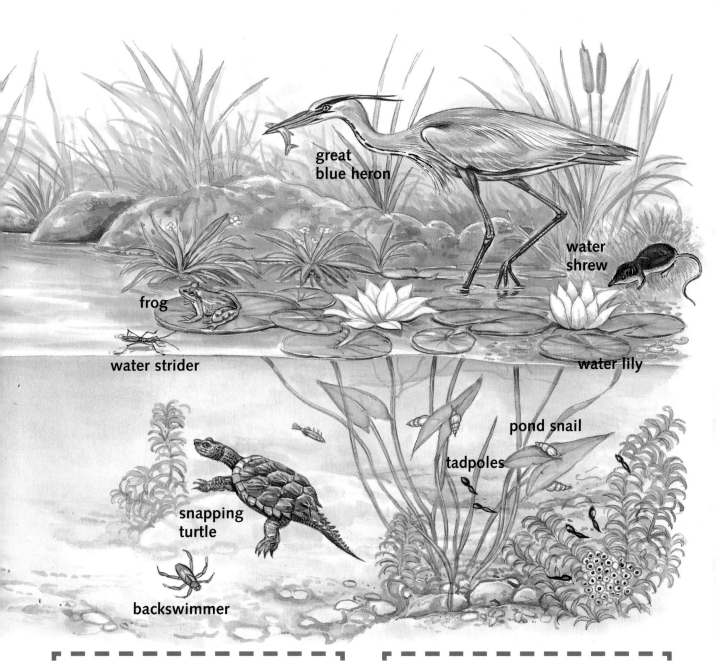

great
blue heron

water
shrew

frog

water strider

water lily

pond snail

tadpoles

snapping
turtle

backswimmer

CREEPERS AND CRAWLERS

Nearly half of the 25 major types of bugs in the world live in ponds. Most feed on algae and plants.

HUNGRY ANIMALS

Fish, frogs, and snakes live in and around ponds. They make good meals for roaming **predators**, such as herons.

Plants and Algae

Ponds contain many types of plants, such as water lilies, duckweed, and hornworts. Ponds are also home to simple plantlike living things called algae. On the microscopic level, billions of **bacteria** live in ponds. They make a pond stink of rotten eggs because they give off a smelly gas as they break down old leaves in the water.

Some algae form long strands that are only one-cell thick.

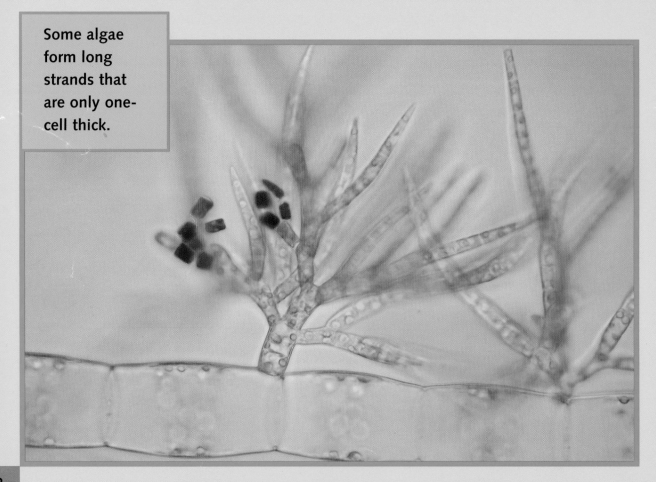

Tangled strands of algae make slimy green clumps, known as pond scum.

Rushes and reeds surround the pond. The water gets its color from millions of tiny green algae.

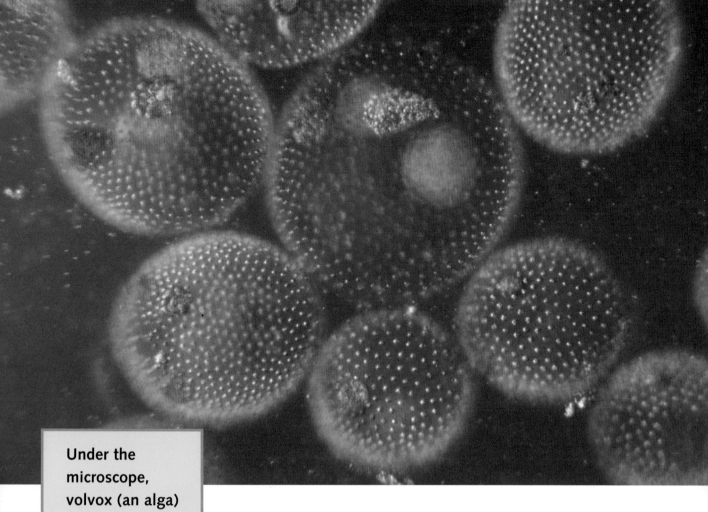

Under the microscope, volvox (an alga) looks like spiky balls. Daughter cells live inside each globe.

Duckweed leaves have air-filled pockets that act like water wings.

Food Factories

Plants and algae gather energy from sunlight to make food. They are highly efficient food factories. Duckweed floats across ponds. Its leaves make a bright green carpet on the surface of the pond. The duckweed's tiny roots dangle into the water. Simple rooted plants thrive at the edges of a pond and in its depths. These plants, such as waterweed and hornwort, live completely underwater and have finely divided leaves. Plants that put out leaves on the pond's surface usually have broad, flat leaves instead.

WATER LILIES

The water lily has large, round leaves, which push up through the water in a tight roll. At the surface, the leaves unfurl, pushing other plants aside. The surface of the lily's leaf is smooth and waxy, but the underside, where snails graze and lay their eggs, is slimy. Water lilies produce spectacular flowers, which open only on sunny days. The flowers do not open if it is raining. Rain would fill the flower and make the bloom sink.

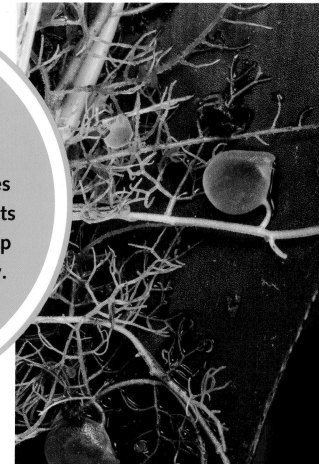

Gotcha!

Unlike most plants, the bladderwort is a meat eater! It dangles small traps, called bladders, from its feathery leaves into the water. When pond insects swim past, the bladderwort's trap snaps open, sucking in its **prey**. The plant **digests** its catch to get extra nutrients.

Creepers and Crawlers

Ponds are home to hundreds of bugs. One of the most useful in any pond is the water flea, or daphnia, although it is only the size of a poppy seed. It uses its feelers as flippers to push itself through the water as it gobbles up algae and keeps pond water clear. The flea is also a meal for most of the small pond creatures.

The water snail has a tightly coiled shell. It lives in ponds and rivers.

The mouth of a mosquito is a long feeding tube that can pierce skin to get a drink of blood.

Cover your arms and legs when you visit a pond—ponds are a favorite haunt of biting insects, such as mosquitoes.

Snails and Clams

Pond snails eat algae, too. Some of these snails have to breathe at the surface, traveling up plant stems for gulps of air. The great pond snail floats upside down at the surface and eats water lilies. Most freshwater snails are **hermaphrodites**. Each adult has both male and female reproductive parts, so all snails can lay eggs. In pond mud, the fingernail clam filters the water for edible scraps. Fingernail clams sometimes grab the toes of a passing toad or newt to hitch a ride.

Worms live in pond mud. They eat rotting plant materials—and each other!

Pond snails fix their hundreds of eggs to a stem in a protective bag of gel.

Bloodworms are midge larvae. The worms are often sold in pet shops as fish food.

Grubs in the Mud

Early in the year, the pond is full of young insects called **larvae**. Many flying insects, such as mosquitoes and dragonflies, have water-living larvae. Mosquito larvae dangle upside down from the surface to breathe. Tiny midge larvae come in many shapes and colors, from the bright, red bloodworms, which swim like snakes, to phantoms, which are see-through. Both grubs live in tiny ponds and puddles, where few predators lurk.

Slimy Vampires

Leeches are slimy worms with a bad reputation, but not all of them are bloodsuckers. Some eat smaller worms. Leeches spend most of their time under rocks or in the mud at the bottom of the pond. Blood-sucking leeches grow big on a single meal and take up to six months to digest it.

The diving beetle larva has mighty pincers. It uses them to stab prey.

Killer Grubs

The mud at the bottom of the pond is full of fearsome predators. The larvae of dragonflies and diving beetles are the most dangerous of them all, growing up to 2 inches (5 cm) long. Both have large pincers for grabbing other larvae, tadpoles, and even the occasional small fish. The dragonfly larva has a spiked lower lip, called a mask, which it can use to snatch its prey.

Dragonfly larvae, also called **nymphs**, spend up to three years fattening up in the pond before emerging for a brief summer as beautiful flying adults, to mate and lay eggs.

Backswimmers naturally float; water boatmen have to swim to the surface.

Row, Row, Row the Boat

Water boatmen and backswimmers look like beetles, but they are distant relatives. Instead of jaws they have pointed beaks. The boatman uses its beak to vacuum through the mud on bottom of the pond. The backswimmer has a sharp beak, which it uses to stab surface prey from below.

Water scorpions are not related to desert scorpions. These pond bugs have long tails, which they use as breathing tubes, and large claws, which they use to grab passing prey.

Backswimmers can stab a human finger. The bite is not poisonous—but it really hurts!

A water boatman uses its two feathery legs to push through the water, just like a rower using a pair of oars.

Beetling About

Adult diving beetles are strong swimmers and expert hunters. Like their larvae, they have pincer jaws for grappling small fish and other prey. As they dive, they carry air in the hairs on their **abdomen** and under their wing cases. The air helps the beetles rise back to the surface. Another water beetle, the great silver beetle, carries a bubble of air. The adults eat only plants, but the larvae are fierce predators.

Mayflies live three years as larvae but only a few hours as adults.

Common in ponds, diving beetles can grow up to 1.5 inches (3.8 cm) long.

Spring into Action

Springtails look like tiny gray-black flecks. They sometimes gather on the pond's surface, where they graze on floating particles. They provide a source of food for other small animals, such as young frogs and toads. A flick of their "spring" tails can propel them an inch or two (up to 5 cm) into the air—a mighty leap for an insect that is only 1/16 inch (0.16 cm) long.

Springtails group together in "rafts" that look like ash floating on the water's surface.

WALKING ON WATER

Surface tension occurs when a liquid, like water, meets a gas, such as air. It acts as an elastic skin on the pond's surface. Surface tension is not strong enough to support bigger animals, such as salamanders. The stretchy skin does let small, light animals, such as water striders (left) and swamp spiders, walk on the water's surface without getting wet. Water striders eat any wriggling animal they can catch on the pond's surface. The insects pinpoint their prey using their four back feet, which pick up ripples on the pond.

Spiders and Whirligigs

The swamp spider also uses the pond's surface tension to detect its prey. It sits with its forelegs dangling on the water's surface. When it detects the wriggling of its prey, it lunges into the water, gathers its victim into its jaws, and drags it back onto its perch to eat.

The whirligig beetle lives on the surface of the pond. It spins around to look for food. Both of its eyes are split in two. The top halves look for overhead threats, so the beetle can dive into the water to hide. The bottom halves watch below, and if danger looms, the beetle flies to safety.

The swamp spider is a little less than 2 inches (5 cm) across—legs included. It has a poisonous bite.

Dragonflies can fly at speeds of nearly 18 miles (29 km) per hour. Dragonfly adults mate in midair.

Pond Show-offs

When it is time for a dragonfly larva to leave the pond, it crawls up a stalk, where an amazing change takes place. After a few hours, an adult dragonfly wriggles out of its old body and unfurls two brand-new pairs of wings.

There are two different families of dragonflies: darners and skimmers. Darners hover for long periods, scanning for prey, and have long, thin abdomens. Skimmers are stubbier. They prefer to rest on a lookout point (a twig or a leaf), then dart out to snatch food or defend their patch.

The largest prehistoric insect was a dragonfly. This giant had a 2-foot (0.6-m) wingspan. It lived 300 million years ago.

Male dragonflies, such as this darner, have claspers at the end of their abdomen to grip females.

Hungry Animals

Big animals rarely live in a pond all year round, but some hunters, such as water snakes and mink, stop by for a snack, and frogs and toads return to ponds to mate. Small ponds in the wild cannot support very big fish. Anything much larger than a minnow or stickleback would soon eat up all the other animals.

The male stickleback guards its nest until the eggs inside hatch.

Northern water snakes produce a powerful skunklike smell when they are threatened by a predator.

Northern water snakes like to bask on rocks or overhanging branches.

The American bullfrog returns to a pond to mate. It keeps damp in the muddy shallows.

Spring Is Here

Frogs and toads arrive at the pond in spring to mate and **spawn**. Frogs are noisiest when they are courting. The special stretchy sacs around the males' vocal cords can make a range of calls to attract a mate. Frogs' eggs form large slimy clumps, which can contain a mixture of eggs from many different females.

Very few of the thousands of tadpoles in each pond become adults. Tadpoles are easy prey for hundreds of other creatures, including the bigger insect larvae, swamp spiders, fish, turtles, and visiting birds.

Unlike frogs, toads lay their eggs in strings up to 6 feet (1.8 m) long.

IT'S A FROG'S LIFE

These **amphibians** lay thousands of eggs with a black center and a see-through, gel-like coating (1). The tadpoles hatch from the eggs and swim by wriggling their tails. They have **gills**, and at first they look like baby fish, but with rounder bodies (2). By early summer, the tadpoles have sprouted back legs and webbed feet (3). They soon grow forelegs and lose their tails. Now they are like miniature adults. In a few months, they are ready to mate (4), and the cycle begins again.

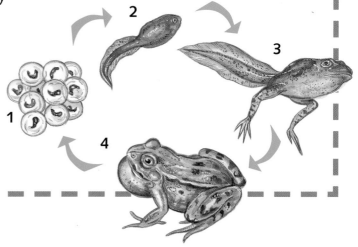

Hop to It!

The tadpoles that do grow up into frogs and toads leave the pond to find a safe, damp spot where there are plenty of bugs to eat. They do not travel far, because they need to keep their skins moist to help them breathe. Some only return to their ponds to breed, although some frogs risk being icebound and stay in the pond through winter.

Toads spend cold winters in a deep sleep called hibernation.

Toads with Tails

Salamanders are amphibians, like frogs and toads. The main difference is that salamanders keep their tails as adults. Some types of salamanders, such as newts, attract mates underwater, with displays of tail-wagging from the male. Female newts lay one egg at a time, taking great care to hide each one in a folded leaf. Newts eat insects, worms, and tadpoles—often their own!

Newts swim by wriggling their bodies, just like fish.

The red-spotted newt lives on land as an adult but returns to a pond to breed.

Kicking Up a Stink

Many types of turtles live in or by freshwater ponds. Most prefer muddy shallows where they can reach air with their nostrils. Stinkpot turtles are rarely longer than 6 inches (15 cm), but snapping turtles grow to three times that length. Snapping turtles eat small pond animals, including birds, as well as plants and algae. Softshell turtles have fleshy lips, which cover their beaks, and a tube-shaped nose, which they use like a snorkel.

The shell of a snapping turtle is actually soft. This **reptile** relies on its sharp beak for self-defense.

Mudpuppies are a type of salamander. They never leave the water or lose their gills.

The great blue heron will feed whole fish to its brood of hungry chicks.

Patient Hunters

Herons visit quiet ponds, where they stand still for hours waiting for a meal to come within striking distance of their long, sharp beaks. They stab underwater for fish and also pick off frogs and toads. Their long necks distinguish them from most other birds. Herons are the only birds to fly with their neck bent back and their heads tucked between their shoulders.

The great blue heron has a 6-foot (1.8-m) wingspan and can weigh up to 8 pounds (3.5 kg).

Furry and Fearsome

Mink are fearsome hunters. They gobble up bigger prey, including fish, mice, frogs, snakes, salamanders, bird eggs, and small water birds or chicks. Their feet are partly webbed to help them swim well. Mink are especially good at catching muskrats, often making their dens in the muskrat burrows. They are hunted by foxes and sometimes owls, but their biggest enemy is a shortage of food. Mink mate between January and March and give birth to a litter of around four kits (babies) a month later.

The ermine (a type of weasel) has fur that turns white in fall to make it invisible against the winter snow when hunting.

Just like other **mammals**, mink kits feed on their mother's milk. After that, they hunt on land and in water.

Life in Your Own Pond

You don't have to find a pond in the wild to enjoy pond life. It will come and find you, if you collect some rainwater in an old pail or bucket. Just leave the water standing outside for more than a week in summer, and you will begin to notice the pond life arriving. Scoop a glass full of water from your bucket. You will find that

Mosquito larvae hang from the pond's surface. If disturbed, they wriggle away.

Goldfish and koi carp in ornamental ponds will eat most other small pond creatures.

TOP TIPS FOR POND WATCHERS

1 Always approach a wild pond carefully; animals that you can see from a distance are likely to hide if you move nearer.

2 Never go near a pond alone. Even shallow water can be very dangerous.

3 Many of the animals in this book are best viewed at night. Ask an adult to take you to a pond with a flashlight.

the water looks greenish. That is because algae has moved in, and if you are lucky, you may see dark green strands of algae, too. If you use a bigger container, such as an old bathtub, water striders flying past will drop in to eat the insects trapped on the surface.

After a little while, midges and mosquitoes will leave tiny, wriggling larvae in the water. If you do not want to get bitten, now might be the time to pour out your bucket pond and go looking for the real thing!

Glossary

abdomen The rear part of an insect's body.

algae Simple, plantlike life-forms.

amphibians Animals that live both on land and in water. Frogs, toads, and newts are amphibians.

bacteria Microscopic, single-celled life-forms.

digests Breaks up food in the body to extract its nutrients.

gills Feathery organs used for breathing underwater.

hermaphrodites Animals with both male and female parts.

larvae Immature (young) insects.

mammals Warm-blooded, hairy animals that suckle their young.

nymphs The larvae of certain insects, such as dragonflies.

predators Animals that hunt other animals for food.

prey An animal hunted and eaten by others animals.

reptile A cold-blooded, scaly, air-breathing animal, such as a turtle, snake, or lizard.

spawn A mass of frog, toad, or fish eggs.

Index

01|11